Contents

KU-274-912

Words written in bold, **like this,** are explained in the Glossary.

 Find out more about space at www.heinemannexplore.co.uk.

Looking at the Earth

We all live on the planet Earth. Look around you, what can you see? You only see a tiny part of the Earth because it is so large.

From the Earth we can only see a small part of our planet.

This is a different view of the Earth. It is what the Earth looks like from space.

A big blue marble

Twelve **astronauts** have seen the Earth from the surface of the Moon. One astronaut said that from space, the Earth looks like a big blue marble.

A view of the Earth from the Moon.

**Looking at the Earth from the
cargo bay of a space shuttle.**

Hundreds of astronauts have seen the
Earth from spacecrafts and space
stations. Many people on Earth have seen
satellite images of the Earth, too.

Earth's axis

Although we cannot feel it, the Earth is always moving. It spins on its **axis**. It takes 24 hours for the Earth to turn around once on its axis.

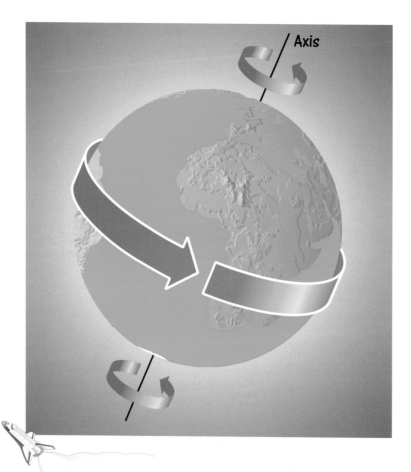

Axis

The Earth's axis is an imaginary pole that runs through the middle of the Earth.

As the Earth spins, people on Earth look out at different parts of space. Their view of the sky will change as the Earth spins.

As the Earth spins, different parts move in and out of the Sun's light.

Day and night

From space, it is easy to see which part of the Earth has sunlight on it. The edge of sunlight is where day is beginning or ending.

It is daytime for the side of Earth with sunlight on it.

As the Earth spins, day changes to night and night to day for different places on the Earth. While it is night on one side of the Earth, it is day on the other.

As day is beginning for some places on Earth, it is night time in others.

 Photographs

Satellites take pictures of the Earth from space. Scientists use these photographs to learn more about the Earth.

Scientists look at satellite photos of the Earth to see changes on the Earth in its temperature and weather.

Scientists can work out what areas on the Earth are cold or hot, and work out what the weather might be like next.

Some satellite photographs show buildings and streets. These are used to make maps. Other satellite photographs show changes in the weather. These are used to help **forecast** the weather.

13

The Earth is covered with a layer of **gas** called the **atmosphere**. It is what people, plants and animals breathe. From space, the Earth's atmosphere looks thin and blue.

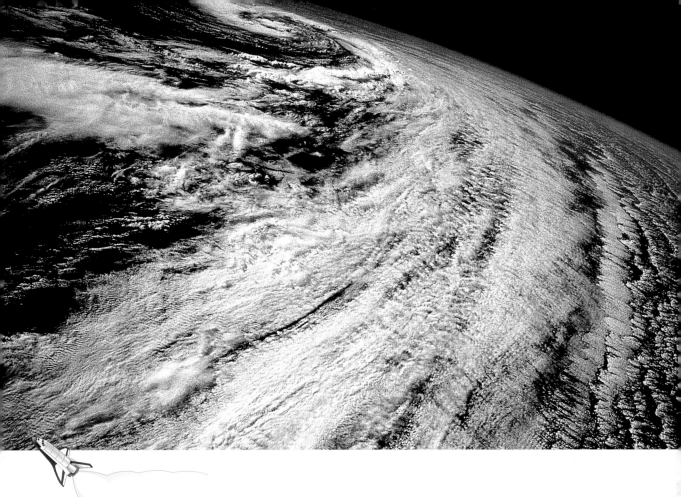

The shape and type of cloud can help show what type of weather a place will have.

The atmosphere is full of white clouds. The clouds change and sometimes disappear as they move across the Earth. **Meteorologists** watch the changes to **forecast** the weather.

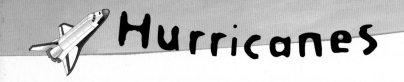

Hurricanes

A hurricane is a type of storm. The strong winds and heavy rains can damage buildings and trees. **Meteorologists** use pictures from space to **forecast** when a hurricane will happen.

eye of the hurricane

This is what a hurricane looks like
from space. The hurricane clouds
spin around the hurricane's eye. The
eye of the hurricane is not stormy.

Satellites take photographs of the Earth's seas and oceans to show their different **temperatures**. The temperature of water in the oceans affects weather patterns on the Earth.

This satellite photograph shows temperatures as different colours. The red is hot, the purple is cool.

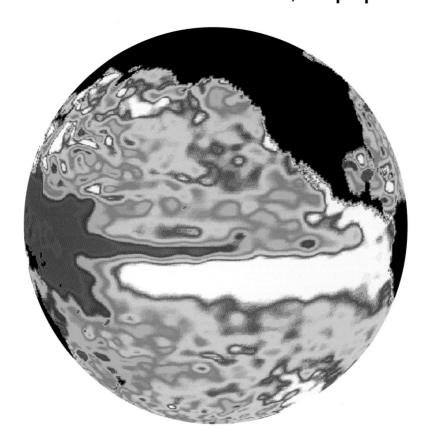

This is a satellite picture of an iceberg near Antarctica.

Some oceans are covered with ice. The Arctic Ocean is covered with ice all year. Photos of the Arctic Ocean can show how the ice changes.

19

Continents

A continent is a very large area of land. Sometimes continents include many countries. The Earth has seven continents. From space, each continent is easy to see.

In this **satellite** photograph, North and South America can be seen.

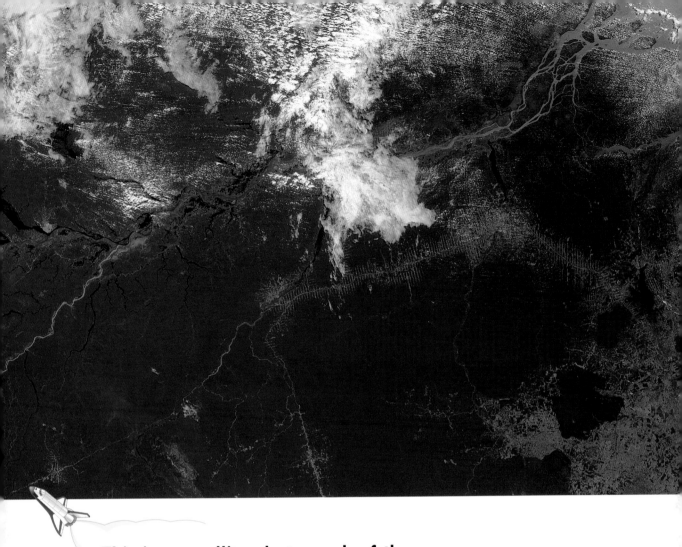

This is a satellite photograph of the Amazon Rainforest in South America.

Satellites can take photographs of a whole continent, or just a small part. From space, a forest on a continent looks like a green carpet.

Deserts and mountains

Deserts are places on the Earth that do not get much rain. Many deserts are sandy and have very few plants growing in them.

This is a **satellite** photograph of the Sahara desert in Africa. The ridges are sand dunes.

This is a satellite photograph of the Himalayas. The white part of this photo is snow.

Mountains form the tallest parts of the Earth. On the Earth, mountains tower above us, but from space, they look like wrinkled paper.

Volcanoes

A volcano looks like a mountain. But hot **gases**, melted rock and ash flow out of volcanoes when they **erupt**. Some volcano eruptions can be seen from space.

Lava is liquid rock that is pushed to the Earth's surface when a volcano erupts.

Satellites in space take photographs of the clouds of ash that come out of volcanoes. These clouds of smoke are carried in the wind and may be seen for days.

A cloud of smoke is erupting from Kliuchevskoi, a volcano in Russia.

City lights

At night, cities make a lot of light because of buildings and street lights. People in cities cannot see many stars in the night sky because of the **light pollution**.

City lights can be seen from space. Light areas show where cities are across the Earth. Dark places are areas that do not have large cities in them.

Looking from Space

A **space probe** travelled to Mars to take pictures on the planet. It also took a photograph of the Earth.

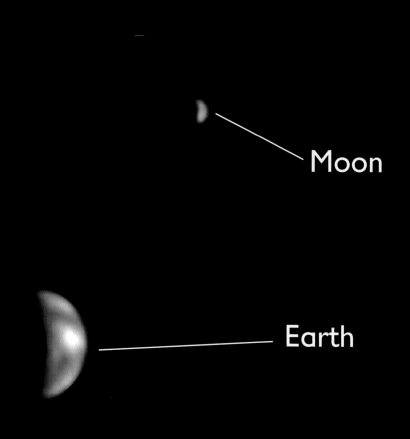

Moon

Earth

If a **satellite** near the planet Jupiter could take a photograph of the Earth, it would only look like a tiny dot of light.

From Jupiter, the Earth would look very similar to the stars we can see at night.

Amazing Earth facts

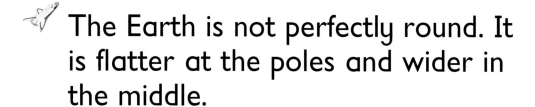

The Earth is not perfectly round. It is flatter at the poles and wider in the middle.

The first **satellite** image of the Earth used for **forecasting** weather was sent from space on 1 April, 1960.

You can see satellites that take photographs of the Earth moving across the night sky. They look like tiny points of light.

 Find out more about space at www.heinemannexplore.co.uk.

Glossary

astronaut person who goes into space

atmosphere layer of gas around a planet

axis an imaginary pole that runs through Earth, from the North Pole to the South Pole

erupt to burst out of

forecast guess what is going to happen in the future

gas air-like material that is not solid or liquid

light pollution light that does not allow the night sky to be clearly seen

meteorologist scientist who studies the weather

satellite object that moves around a planet or a moon

space probe spacecraft used to explore space

temperature how hot or cold something is

More books and websites

Day and Night (Nature's Patterns), Anita Ganeri (Heinemann Library, 2004)
The Sun (Space Explorer), Patricia Whitehouse (Heinemann Library, 2004)
Space Equipment (Space Explorer), Patricia Whitehouse (Heinemann Library, 2004)
Weather Patterns (Nature's Patterns), Monica Hughes (Heinemann Library, 2004)

www.esa.int
www.nasa.gov/audience/forkids

Index